Salads and Snacks

by Marion Howells

CONTENTS

Published by Sharon Publications
Distributed by Sharon Marketing
Fort Lee, New Jersey
Under arrangement with Ottenheimer Publishers, Inc.

MEAT SALADS

Introduction

The story of salads begins with the ancient Egyptians who served raw greens with oil and vinegar mixed with Oriental spices. The Romans are credited with popularizing salads—in fact one legend has it that Augustus Caesar built an altar to honor the healthful qualities of lettuce.

Salads are the most versatile of foods. In the following recipes you will find salads suitable to serve as hors d'oeuvre, as a regular course, as an accompaniment to other foods and as dessert. No other dish you make offers such possibilities for your imagination—in blending colors, flavors and textures.

Select the best quality salad greens available. Prepare them carefully—pat them dry with a soft towel and refrigerate as soon as possible after purchase to ensure crispness.

Whatever the salad, there is always a dressing to improve it, but add the dressing at the last minute unless the recipe suggests otherwise.

In the second section you will find a selection of snacks—for quick lunches, late-night suppers, or just a bite between meals.

Ham and Pineapple Salad

This salad of pasta and ham makes a complete luncheon dish (Serves 4)

½ cup shell or other small pasta
3 tablespoons mayonnaise (see p. 24)
1 green pepper, seeded and chopped
4 large slices cooked ham
lettuce
4 rings pineapple
2 tomatoes

1. Cook the pasta in boiling salted water for 10 minutes. Drain well.

2. While still warm, add mayonnaise, green pepper and seasoning, then set aside to get quite cold.

3. Place a spoonful of the mixture on one half of each slice of ham, fold the other half over.

4. Arrange on a bed of lettuce and place a ring of pineapple on each slice of ham. Garnish with wedges of tomato.

Swiss Ham Salad

A simple salad of ham and Gruyère cheese (Serves 4—5)

3/4 lb cooked ham, cut in thick slices and diced
3/4 lb Gruyère cheese, diced
6 tablespoons olive oil
2 tablespoons white wine vinegar
salt, freshly ground black pepper
Romaine lettuce or curly endive
finely chopped parsley or fresh herbs

1. Combine the ham and cheese in a bowl.

2. Make a dressing with the oil, vinegar, salt and pepper, pour over the ham and cheese and toss lightly. Refrigerate and leave about 1 hour to marinate.

3. Arrange the lettuce in a salad bowl, pile the ham and cheese in the center and sprinkle with parsley or herbs.

Rainbow Salad

A colorful salad of ham, cottage cheese, apple, carrots and hard-boiled eggs (Serves 4)

1/4 lb cooked ham, diced
1 cup cottage cheese
a pinch of cayenne pepper
1/4 teaspoon salt
1/2 cucumber
4 stalks celery, chopped
2 red dessert apples, cored and
    chopped but not peeled
2 carrots, grated
2 tablespoons lemon juice
lettuce
2 hard-boiled eggs
parsley or watercress

DRESSING
1/2 cup yoghurt
1 teaspoon lemon juice
a pinch of garlic salt
1 teaspoon prepared mustard
black pepper, paprika pepper
Combine all ingredients

1. Combine the ham, cottage cheese, pepper and salt.

2. Arrange some thin slices of cucumber around the edge of a large platter and cut the rest into 1/4 inch dice.

3. Put the diced cucumber, celery, apples and carrots into a bowl, add the lemon juice and mix well. Arrange on the platter, put some lettuce leaves in the center and place the ham and cheese mixture on top.

4. Cut the eggs in halves lengthways and arrange on top. Place a sprig of parsley or watercress in the center.

5. Serve with the dressing.

Ham Rolls

Slices of ham, filled with a mixture of rice flavored with curry powder and blended with apple and onion (Serves 4)

1/2 cup rice
chicken stock or water
1 bay leaf
1 tablespoon oil
2 tablespoons butter
1/2 small onion, peeled and finely chopped
1 small apple, peeled, cored and chopped
1.1/2 teaspoons curry powder
4 tablespoons light cream
grated rind of 1 lemon
2 tablespoons lemon juice
2 tablespoons chopped cooked ham
2 tablespoons chopped red pepper
8 slices cooked ham
lettuce
black olives and canned pimento for garnish

1. Cook the rice in boiling stock or salted water with the bay leaf. Drain, and while still hot stir in the oil, making sure the rice is well coated.

2. Heat the butter in a skillet, add onion and apple and cook for 5 minutes. Stir in curry powder, cook for a few minutes. Remove from the heat, add cream, grated lemon rind and juice, chopped ham, red pepper, and rice. Set aside for about 1 hour to chill.

3. Roll this mixture in slices of ham and secure with a cocktail stick or toothpick if necessary.

4. Arrange on a bed of lettuce and garnish with black olives and strips of pimento.

Chicken Salad with Lychees

The lychees and mandarins add color and interest to this salad
(Serves 5—6)

3 cups cooked diced chicken
2—3 stalks celery, chopped
1 green pepper, chopped
3/4 cup French dressing (see p. 26)
salad greens
1 can lychees
1 small can mandarins

DRESSING
3/4 cup mayonnaise (see p. 24)
1/4 cup sour cream
2 teaspoons curry powder
2 tablespoons grated onion
2 tablespoons chopped parsley

1. Combine the chicken, celery and green pepper. Add salt, pepper and the French dressing. Toss lightly together and chill for about 1/2 hour.

2. Arrange some salad greens round a large platter and pile the chicken mixture in the center.

3. Drain the lychees and mandarins. Place a mandarin segment in each lychee and arrange round the edge or down the center.

4. Blend all the ingredients for the dressing together, chill well and serve the dressing separately.

1 cut clove of garlic
1 cup shredded lettuce
1 cup shredded Romaine
1 cup shredded escarole
1 small bunch watercress
1/2 green pepper, seeded and cut into rings
1/2 can luncheon meat, shredded
1/4 lb American cheese, cut into strips
3 hard-boiled eggs, cut into wedges
French dressing, about 1/2 cup (see p. 26)

Luncheon Salad Bowl

A variety of salad greens is used for this salad, and the ingredients can be varied to suit your taste. The salad should be served as soon as it is prepared (Serves 5–6)

1. Rub a wooden salad bowl with the cut clove of garlic.

2. Arrange all the ingredients in the bowl. Add the dressing and toss lightly until all the ingredients are coated.

Turkey and Pomegranate Salad

2 cups cooked turkey, cut into cubes
2–3 stalks celery, chopped
seeds from 1 large ripe pomegranate
1 cup blanched chopped almonds
salt, black pepper
mayonnaise (see p. 24)
lettuce
2 slices pineapple, cut into wedges

The shiny red seeds of the pomegranate add color and interest to this salad. Try not to bruise the seeds while preparing the salad (Serves 5–6)

1. Combine the turkey, celery, pomegranate seeds and almonds. Season carefully with salt and freshly ground black pepper.

2. Add enough mayonnaise to moisten and toss all lightly together.

3. Serve on a bed of lettuce and garnish with wedges of pineapple.

Macaroni Salad (see p. 9)

Chicken Salad

This salad, topped with grapes and crunchy almonds, makes a good party dish (Serves 5–6)

1/4 lb mushrooms
1/2 cup French dressing(see p. 26)
1 large iceberg lettuce
1.1/2 cups diced cooked chicken
1 can artichoke hearts, drained and cut in halves
1 small red pepper, seeded and cut into strips
1/2 lb cooked green beans, sliced
1 cup grapes, halved and seeded
1/4 cup toasted flaked almonds

1. Wash and slice the mushrooms and place in a shallow bowl. Pour the French dressing over them and set aside for 1 hour, stirring occasionally.

2. Wash the lettuce, discarding outer leaves, and line a deep salad bowl or large platter.

3. Combine the chicken, artichoke hearts, red pepper and beans. Add the mushrooms and the dressing, season to taste, and toss all lightly together. Refrigerate until ready to serve, then spoon the chicken mixture over the lettuce.

4. Sprinkle with grapes and toasted almonds.

Avocado and Chicken Salad

A mixture of chicken and orange arranged in avocado pear halves. (Serves 6)

3 ripe avocado pears
2 tablespoons orange juice
1 cup diced cooked chicken
1–2 stalks celery, diced
3 oranges
1/4 cup mayonnaise (see p. 24)
a pinch of paprika pepper
1 tablespoon chopped pimento
salad greens

1. Peel avocados, remove the stones and scoop out some of the flesh. Brush the avocados with orange juice.

2. Cut the scooped out avocado flesh into small pieces and place in a bowl with the chicken and celery.

3. Peel and section 2 of the oranges, removing seeds and white pith. Cut into small pieces and add to the chicken and celery mixture.

4. Combine the mayonnaise with the paprika, add salt to taste and blend with the chicken.

5. Fill the avocado halves and sprinkle with chopped pimento. Serve on a bed of salad greens and garnish with sections of the remaining orange.

Potato and Frankfurter Salad

(Serves 4)

1 lb potatoes
6–8 scallions, chopped
1 teaspoon chopped parsley
cream dressing (see p. 25)
1 lettuce
4 frankfurters
4 slices cooked ham
2 hard-boiled eggs, quartered
3–4 tomatoes

1. Cook, peel and dice the potatoes. Add onion and parsley and while potatoes are still warm add 3–4 tablespoons cream dressing. Toss lightly and set aside to chill.

2. Put the potato in the center of a platter lined with lettuce leaves.

3. Put a frankfurter on each slice of ham and roll up. Arrange the ham rolls around the dish and garnish with hard-boiled eggs and tomatoes.

VEGETABLE SALADS

Raw Mushroom Salad

(Serves 5—6)

1. Remove the stalks from the mushrooms, wash and dry the caps and cut into slices. Arrange in a shallow salad bowl.

2. Blend the lemon juice and oil, add salt and pepper to taste and pour over the mushrooms. Toss carefully and set aside to chill for at least 1/2 hour.

3. Before serving, sprinkle with the chives and parsley.

VARIATION
Prepare the mushrooms as above and add 3—4 tablespoons mayonnaise to the lemon and oil dressing.

1 lb button mushrooms
juice of 1 lemon
8 tablespoons olive oil
salt, freshly ground black pepper
1 teaspoon finely chopped chives
1 teaspoon finely chopped parsley

Peanut Crunch Slaw

A coleslaw mixture with a crunchy topping of toasted peanuts and cheese
(Serves 6—7)

1. Combine cabbage and celery. Sprinkle with a little salt and pepper and set aside to chill.

2. Combine all ingredients for the dressing, season and chill.

3. When required for use, brown the peanuts in the butter and stir in the cheese.

4. Toss the vegetables and dressing together and sprinkle the nuts and cheese on top.

4 cups shredded white cabbage
1 cup diced celery

DRESSING
1/2 cup sour cream
1/2 cup mayonnaise (see p. 24)
1/4 cup chopped scallions
1/4 cup green chopped pepper
1/4 cup chopped cucumber

TOPPING
1/2 cup salted peanuts, coarsely
    chopped
1 tablespoon butter
2 tablespoons grated Parmesan cheese

Coleslaw with Almonds

(Serves 4—5)

1. Wash and drain the cabbage, discard outer leaves and hard stalk.

2. Shred the cabbage finely and mix with the celery, cucumber, green pepper and onion.

3. Mix the mayonnaise and vinegar, add salt and pepper to taste and pour over the vegetables. Toss with two forks until the vegetables are evenly coated.

4. Put into a serving dish and sprinkle with toasted almonds.

1/2 medium-size white cabbage
2 stalks celery, chopped
1/2 cucumber, thinly sliced
1/2 green pepper, shredded
1 onion, peeled and finely chopped
2/3 cup mayonnaise (see p. 24)
1 tablespoon vinegar
1/4 cup toasted browned almonds

Pasta Slaw

1/4 cup mayonnaise (see p. 24)
1 tablespoon sour cream
1 tablespoon vinegar
2 teaspoons sugar
1 cup pasta, cooked (any kind)
1 cup finely shredded white cabbage
3 tablespoons grated carrot
3 tablespoons diced green pepper

A good salad to serve with any kind of cold meat or poultry (Serves 4—5)

1. Make a dressing with the mayonnaise, sour cream, vinegar and sugar.

2. Add the pasta and vegetables and toss lightly, but be sure all the ingredients are well coated with the dressing.

Salad Andalouse

A simple salad of rice with tomatoes and pimentos. A good way of using left-over rice (Serves 4)

1 cup cooked rice
4 tomatoes, peeled and cut into quarters
2 canned pimentos, cut into thin strips
1 clove garlic, crushed
1/2 onion, peeled and finely chopped
French dressing (see page 26)
finely chopped parsley

1. Combine the rice, tomatoes, pimento, garlic and onion. Add seasoning if required.

2. Add enough French dressing to coat all ingredients well but avoid adding excess dressing.

3. Sprinkle with parsley before serving.

Macaroni Salad

A salad of macaroni, cheese, gherkins and peas blended with mayonnaise. Excellent as an accompaniment to any broiled meat (Serves 6—see picture, p. 6)

2 cups shell or ring macaroni
2 tablespoons butter
1 cup cubed Cheddar cheese
1 cup sliced gherkins
1/2 cup very finely chopped onion
2 cups cooked peas
1/2 cup mayonnaise (see p. 24)
seasoning
lettuce

1. Cook the macaroni in boiling salted water, drain well, add the butter and toss lightly.

2. Add cheese, gherkins, onion and peas.

3. Stir in the mayonnaise and blend carefully, making sure the macaroni is well mixed with the mayonnaise.

4. Check the seasoning and set aside to chill.

5. Serve individually in lettuce leaves or on a bed of shredded lettuce.

Stuffed Tomatoes

A good accompaniment to cold chicken or turkey (Serves 4)

1. Peel the tomatoes after plunging them into boiling water for 1 minute and then in cold water.

2. Cut in half crossways and remove the seeds and pulp. Cover loosely with foil and chill in the refrigerator until required.

8 firm ripe tomatoes
2 ripe avocado pears
juice of 1 lemon
1 tablespoon onion juice
salt, black pepper
a pinch of chili powder
4 tablespoons finely chopped celery or green pepper
1 tablespoon finely chopped parsley

3. Peel the avocados, remove the seed and mash well with a wooden spoon. Add lemon juice, salt, pepper, chili powder and celery or green pepper. Set aside to chill.

4. When ready to use, fill the tomato halves with the avocado mixture and sprinkle with parsley.

Caesar Salad

A plain green salad topped with crispy bacon and bread croûtons (Serves 4–5)

2 small heads Romaine or other lettuce
2 tablespoons butter
1 clove garlic, crushed
2 slices bread, cut into 1/2 inch cubes
2 slices bacon, chopped
grated Parmesan cheese
chopped parsley

DRESSING
1 coddled egg
2/3 cup French dressing (see p. 26)
1 teaspoon salt
1 teaspoon prepared mustard

1. To make the dressing, coddle the egg first by putting it into boiling water for 1 minute and then removing the shell. Then mix well with all the other ingredients.

2. Remove any tough outer leaves from the lettuce, wash and dry well. Break up into pieces, put into a salad bowl, add the dressing and toss lightly.

3. Heat the butter in a skillet, add crushed garlic and cubes of bread and cook until crisp and golden brown. Fry the bacon until crisp, then drain on absorbent paper.

4. Scatter the bacon and croûtons over the salad and sprinkle generously with grated cheese and parsley.

Wilted Lettuce Salad

The waxy texture of Boston lettuce makes it especially suitable for this type of salad (Serves 4)

1 large head Boston lettuce
6 radishes, thinly sliced
1 hard-boiled egg
5–6 slices bacon
1 teaspoon sugar
1/4 cup red wine vinegar
1/4 teaspoon prepared horseradish
1/8 teaspoon black pepper
5–6 scallions, chopped

1. Wash and drain the lettuce and break it up into a salad bowl. Add sliced radishes.

2. Remove the yolk carefully from the hard-boiled egg and set aside. Chop the white of egg and sprinkle over the lettuce.

3. Cook the bacon in a skillet until crisp. Remove, and drain on absorbent paper.

4. Add sugar, vinegar, horseradish and pepper to the bacon drippings in the skillet. Mix well, add scallions and heat until the mixture bubbles, then pour at once over the lettuce. Toss lightly. Add the crumbled bacon and sprinkle with the sieved hard-boiled egg yolk.

Hot Potato Salad

A hot salad of potato, bacon and eggs. Very good to serve with frankfurters (Serves 4)

3 large potatoes
2 tablespoons vinegar
1 teaspoon salt, pepper
1/2 lb bacon, chopped
3 eggs
1/4 cup chopped scallions
lettuce
4 frankfurters

1. Scrub the potatoes, cook in boiling salted water, then drain, peel and cut into dice. Add vinegar, salt and pepper.

2. Fry the bacon until crisp.

3. Hard-boil the eggs.

4. Combine the potatoes, bacon, 2 tablespoons of the bacon fat, chopped eggs and onion and mix well.

5. Serve hot on a bed of lettuce with frankfurters.

Ratatouille Salad

Ratatouille is the well known Provencal dish consisting of a selection of vegetables cooked in oil. Try it this way—served cold as a salad (Serves 4)

2 eggplants
a little coarse salt
olive oil, about 1/2 cup
1 onion, peeled and chopped
1 large red pepper, seeded and cut
    into small pieces
4 tomatoes, peeled and chopped
2 cloves garlic, crushed
12 coriander seeds
chopped basil or parsley

1. Wipe the eggplants, cut into 1/2 inch squares and put into a colander. Sprinkle with coarse salt and leave to drain.

2. Heat some of the oil in a skillet and sauté the onion for about 10 minutes or until it begins to soften. Add a little more oil, put in the eggplant and red pepper, cover and simmer for 30—40 minutes.

3. Add tomatoes, garlic and coriander, and continue to cook until the tomatoes are soft and mushy, adding a little more oil if necessary. Adjust the seasoning, then chill.

4. Drain off any excess oil and sprinkle with basil or parsley.

Hot Macaroni Salad

This is an unusual salad in that it is served hot. It makes a good luncheon dish (Serves 5—6)

1 package (about 7 oz) macaroni
6 slices bacon, diced
2 tablespoons vinegar
1 tablespoon finely chopped onion
1/2 teaspoon salt
1/4 teaspoon pepper
1/3 cup salad cream (see p. 23)
1/2 cup sliced radishes
1/4 cup green chopped pepper
1/4 chopped parsley

1. Cook the macaroni in boiling salted water.

2. While the macaroni is cooking, fry the bacon until crisp then remove from the pan and drain off excess fat from the pan, leaving about 1 tablespoon. Add vinegar, onion and seasoning and bring to boiling point.

3. Add drained macaroni and all the other ingredients and toss lightly.

4. Serve hot with a green salad if desired.

SEAFOOD SALADS

Seafood Medley

1 can tuna fish
1 can crab meat
1 can shrimps
2 tablespoons French dressing (see p. 26)
1 cup diced celery
1/2 cup diced cucumber
6—8 radishes, chopped
1 tablespoon capers
2 tablespoons lemon juice
1/2 cup mayonnaise (see p. 24)
salt, pepper, paprika pepper
lettuce

A quickly prepared salad of seafood, made with celery and cucumber and served on crisp lettuce. Canned shrimps can be replaced with fresh if preferred (Serves 5—6)

1. Drain the tuna and break up into flakes. Add flaked crab meat and shrimps. Stir in the French dressing and set aside to chill for about 15 minutes.

2. Add celery, cucumber, radishes and capers.

3. Blend lemon juice with the mayonnaise, add seasoning to taste and toss all ingredients lightly together.

4. Serve on crisp lettuce.

4 tomatoes, peeled and quartered
2 small green peppers, seeded and
   sliced thinly
4 stalks celery, chopped
1 small cooked beet
2 hard-boiled eggs, cut into quarters
1 can anchovy fillets
1 can tuna fish, drained and flaked
green and black olives

DRESSING
2 tablespoons white wine vinegar
6 tablespoons olive oil
salt, freshly ground black pepper
1/2 teaspoon prepared mustard
1 teaspoon each finely chopped
   tarragon, chives, chervil and parsley

Anchovy and Tuna Salad

(Serves 4)

1. Arrange the tomatoes, green peppers, celery, beet and eggs in a salad bowl or on a large platter.

2. Combine all the ingredients for the dressing together and blend well.

3. Arrange the anchovy fillets, tuna and olives attractively on top and pour the dressing over.

Shrimp and Rice Salad

A main meal salad of shrimps and rice with mushrooms and ham
(Serves 4—5)

2 tablespoons butter
2 small onions, peeled and chopped
   finely
1 cup sliced mushrooms
2 cups cooked rice
1 cup cooked peas
1 small red pepper, seeded and cut
   into strips
2 tablespoons chopped parsley
4 oz cooked ham, cut into strips
1 lb or 1 pint shrimp
French dressing (see p. 26)
lettuce
slices of tomato and cucumber for
   garnish

1. Heat the butter and sauté the onions until lightly browned. Remove from the pan. Add a little more butter if required and fry the mushrooms for 3 minutes.

2. Mix onion, mushroom and any pan juices with the rice. Add peas, red pepper, parsley, ham and shrimps, saving a few for the garnish. Mix lightly and add enough dressing to moisten.

3. Arrange the rice mixture in a ring on a serving dish. Surround with shredded lettuce and put the rest of the lettuce in the centre.

4. Top with the reserved shrimps and arrange alternate slices of tomato and cucumber on the ring of lettuce.

Crab Mayonnaise

A delicious summer luncheon dish. The mayonnaise is flavored with tomato purée, curry powder and honey. Lobster can be served in the same way (Serves 5—6)

1 lb fresh, canned, or frozen crab
  meat
1 tablespoon oil
1 small onion, peeled and chopped
2 teaspoons curry powder
2 teaspoons tomato purée
1 tablespoon clear honey
6 tablespoons red wine
4 tablespoons water
juice of 1/2 lemon
1 cup mayonnaise (see p. 24)
1/2 red or green pepper, cut into strips
black olives
2—3 tomatoes
lettuce

1. Arrange the crab meat in a shallow oval dish.

2. Heat the oil in a skillet, fry the onion for 2—3 minutes then add curry powder and fry for another 2 minutes.

3. Add tomato purée, honey, wine and water. Bring to boiling point, add seasoning and lemon juice. Simmer until the mixture becomes thick and syrupy, then strain and leave to cool.

4. Stir this dressing into the mayonnaise and spoon it over the crab.

5. Arrange the strips of pepper in a lattice pattern over the top, put an olive into each square and slices of tomato around the edge. Chill and serve with crisp lettuce.

Salad Nicoise

2 lettuce hearts
4 tomatoes, peeled, seeded and
  quartered
1/2 Spanish onion, peeled and thinly
  sliced
1 green pepper, seeded and cut into
  strips
8 small radishes
4 stalks celery, sliced
1 can tuna fish
8 anchovy fillets
2 hard-boiled eggs
8 black olives

DRESSING
2 tablespoons white wine vinegar or
  lemon juice
6 tablespoons olive oil
few leaves fresh basil, chopped

A favorite luncheon salad of lettuce, vegetables and tuna fish garnished with anchovy fillets and black olives (Serves 4)

1. Line a salad bowl with the lettuce. Combine the vegetables and arrange in the salad bowl.

2. Combine the ingredients for the dressing, pour over the lettuce and vegetables, and toss lightly.

3. Drain the tuna fish, break it up into fairly large pieces and place them on top.

4. Top with the anchovy fillets and wedges of egg, and dot with olives.

Crab Salad

Fresh crab is best for this salad, but use canned if fresh is not available (Serves 4)

1 cup rice
nutmeg
lemon juice
olive oil
1 can crab claw meat (12 or 16 oz),
  or 1 lb fresh white crab meat
6 black olives, pitted
1 red or green pepper, seeded and cut
  into strips
1/2 clove garlic, crushed
3—4 raw mushrooms, sliced
a few walnuts

1. Cook the rice in boiling salted water until just tender (about 12 minutes). Drain well and while still warm add a good pinch of nutmeg, squeeze of lemon juice and enough oil to moisten.

2. Add crab meat cut into squares, olives, red or green pepper, garlic and mushrooms. Mix lightly together.

3. Arrange in a bowl or on a platter and sprinkle chopped walnuts on top.

EGG & CHEESE SALADS

Egg and Shrimp Mayonnaise

For this attractive salad shrimps are combined with mayonnaise, blended with sour cream, flavored with curry powder and used to coat hard-boiled eggs (Serves 6)

1/2 cup mayonnaise (see p. 24)
1 small carton sour cream
1 teaspoon curry powder
6 hard-boiled eggs
lettuce
1 cup fresh or frozen shrimps
paprika pepper
brown bread or rolls

1. Combine the mayonnaise, sour cream and curry powder and chill for 1 hour.

2. Shell and cut the hard-boiled eggs in halves and arrange rounded side up on crisp lettuce.

3. Fold the shrimps into the mayonnaise and spoon over the eggs. Sprinkle with paprika.

4. Serve with rolls or thinly sliced buttered brown bread.

Cheese and Lettuce Salad

A lettuce stuffed with a mixture of cheese, sour cream and vegetables (Serves 5–6)

1 large firm lettuce
1 package (3 oz) cream cheese
8 oz cottage cheese
2 tablespoons sour cream
2 tablespoons very finely chopped or
    minced onion
1/4 cup chopped green pepper
1/2 cup grated raw carrots
1/4 cup chopped nuts
French dressing (see p. 26)

1. Wash, drain and dry the lettuce. Remove the hard central stalk, making a cavity large enough to hold the cheese mixture.

2. Beat the cream cheese, cottage cheese, sour cream and onion together until soft and creamy, add all the other ingredients and blend well.

3. Stuff the lettuce and chill for several hours. Cut into wedges and serve with French dressing.

Cheese and Fruit Salad

A refreshing salad of cream cheese and fruit. Serve as dessert or as an accompaniment to cold poultry or ham (Serves 4)

1 cup cream or cottage cheese
1/3 cup chopped walnuts
2 rings canned or fresh pineapple,
    chopped
1 iceberg or Romaine lettuce
1 large grapefruit
2 bananas
juice of 1/2 lemon
French dressing (see p. 26)

1. Combine the cheese with the nuts and pineapple.

2. Arrange the lettuce on a platter, reserving some of the heart for garnish. Pile the cheese in the center.

3. Arrange segments of grapefruit and slices of banana brushed with lemon juice around the cheese and tuck pieces of lettuce heart in between.

4. Pour the dressing over the top. If canned pineapple is used, 1 tablespoon pineapple juice can be substituted for 1 tablespoon of the oil in the French dressing.

Salad Provencale

This colorful salad consists of red and green peppers, tomatoes and hard-boiled eggs, garnished with anchovies and black olives (Serves 6)

2 red peppers
2 green peppers
6 firm tomatoes, peeled and thickly sliced
6 hard-boiled eggs
anchovy fillets
black olives
herb dressing (see p. 24)

1. Wash and dry the peppers, then broil them quickly, turning frequently until the skin has charred on all sides. Remove the skin under cold water, then cut the peppers lengthways into 6 or 8 pieces. Wash off the seeds and remove excess fiber, then pat dry.

2. Arrange the slices of tomato in the bottom of a large flat serving dish. Sprinkle with some of the dressing, cover with the pieces of green pepper, sprinkle with more dressing, add the pieces of red pepper and sprinkle again with dressing.

3. Shell and slice the hard-boiled eggs and put on top of the red pepper. Add the rest of the dressing.

4. Arrange anchovy fillets in a lattice pattern on top and place an olive in the center of each square. Chill before serving.

5 MOLDED SALADS

Cheese and Macaroni Salad Ring

An attractive salad suitable to serve alone as a light luncheon dish, or as an accompaniment to cold meat or poultry. Any other pasta can be used in place of the elbow macaroni (Serves 6—9)

1 cup elbow macaroni
1/4 cup French dressing (see p. 26)
2 cups cottage cheese
1/4 cup diced pimento
1/4 cup diced green pepper
2 tablespoons very finely chopped onion
2 tablespoons chopped parsley
lettuce
radishes and stuffed green olives for garnish

1. Cook the macaroni in boiling salted water for about 10 minutes. Drain well and while still warm add the French dressing and mix well. Set aside to chill.

2. Add the other ingredients except lettuce, radishes and olives, mix lightly but thoroughly and press into a quart ring mold. Chill for several hours.

3. When ready to serve, arrange some lettuce on a platter. Loosen the mixture from the side of the mold with a knife and turn out on the lettuce.

4. If the salad is to accompany poultry or meat, cut the meat into neat dice, bind with a little mayonnaise, season, and pile in the center of the macaroni ring.

5. Garnish with radish flowers and slices of olive.

Molded Tuna Salad

1 envelope unflavored gelatine
1/4 cup cold water
3/4 cup hot water
2 tablespoons lemon juice
1 teaspoon prepared mustard
1/4 teaspoon paprika pepper
2 cans (6.1/2—7 oz each) tuna fish
1 cup chopped celery
1/2 cup whipped cream
lettuce

DRESSING
1/2 cup mayonnaise (see p. 24)
1/4 cup finely diced cucumber
1 tablespoon chopped green pepper
1 teaspoon tarragon vinegar
a dash of cayenne pepper

(Serves 5—6)

1. Soften the gelatine in cold water for 5—10 minutes, add hot water and stir until the gelatine has melted. Add lemon juice, mustard, paprika and salt to taste. Set aside to chill until partially set.

2. Add drained and flaked tuna and celery and fold in the whipped cream.

3. Spoon into individual molds and chill until set.

4. Turn out on a bed of lettuce. Combine all the ingredients for the dressing, and serve separately.

Ham Mousse

1 envelope unflavored gelatine
2 tablespoons cold water
1/4 cup white wine vinegar
2 cups finely cubed cooked ham
1 cup finely diced celery
1 tablespoon sugar
1 tablespoon pickle relish
1 teaspoon prepared mustard
1/2 cup whipped cream
lettuce
stuffed olives

HORSERADISH CREAM
3 teaspoons well drained horseradish
1/2 teaspoon salt
3/4 cup whipped cream

A light molded mixture of ham, celery and whipped cream. Makes a good party salad (Serves 4—5)

1. Soften the gelatine in the cold water for about 5 minutes. Add the vinegar and heat over hot water until dissolved.

2. Combine ham, celery, sugar, pickle relish and mustard. Stir in the melted gelatine and whipped cream. Check the seasoning and pour into a mold rinsed in cold water. Chill until set.

3. Unmold on a bed of lettuce and garnish with slices of stuffed olives.

4. Fold the horseradish and salt into the whipped cream, and serve separately.

Molded Chicken Salad

The red and green pepper makes a decorative topping for this salad (Serves 5—6)

1 envelope unflavored gelatine
1/4 cup cold water
1 cup hot chicken stock
2 tablespoons chopped red pepper
2 tablespoons chopped green pepper
2 cups diced cooked chicken
1 tablespoon finely chopped onion
1 cup chopped celery
1 cup cooked rice
1/2 teaspoon salt
1/4 cup French dressing (see p. 26)
1/8 teaspoon paprika pepper
1/2 cup mayonnaise (see p. 24)
lettuce

1. Combine the gelatine and cold water and leave for about 10 minutes to soften. Add hot chicken stock and stir until the gelatine has melted.

2. Rinse a mold with cold water, put in the red and green peppers. Cover with 2 tablespoons of the melted gelatine and refrigerate until set.

3. Mix all ingredients except lettuce and add the remaining gelatine.

4. When the gelatine in the mold is quite firm, spoon the chicken mixture on top and leave until set.

5. Unmold and serve on a bed of lettuce.

Tomato Jellied Ring

A ring of well flavored jellied tomato with noodles. The center can be filled with any meat, poultry or fish mixture (Serves 4–6)

4 cups tomato juice
2 teaspoons salt
1/4 teaspoon freshly ground black pepper
1/4 teaspoon finely chopped basil
1 onion, peeled and finely chopped
2 envelopes gelatine
1/4 cup cold water
2 teaspoons prepared horseradish
2 tablespoons sugar
2 tablespoons lemon juice
1/4 lb elbow macaroni, cooked (or noodles)
lettuce

1. Put the tomato juice, seasoning, basil and onion into a skillet, heat to boiling point, and simmer for 10 minutes. Then strain.

2. Soak the gelatine in the cold water for 5 minutes, add to the hot tomato juice, and stir until dissolved.

3. Add horseradish, sugar and lemon juice, adjust the seasoning to taste, and set aside to chill until the mixture begins to thicken.

4. Stir in the cooked macaroni, and pour into a lightly oiled 9 inch ring mold. Chill until set.

5. Unmold on to shredded lettuce, and fill the center as desired.

Molded Apricot Ring

An attractive ring of apricot gelatine sandwiched with cream cheese and green pepper (Serves 4)

1 can (1 lb 4 oz) apricots
1 cup pineapple juice
1 envelope unflavored gelatine
2 tablespoons water
1 package (3 oz) cream cheese
1 tablespoon whipped cream
1/2 small green pepper, blanched and
    finely chopped
a pinch of paprika pepper
a pinch of salt
watercress or lettuce

1. Drain the apricots, finely chop enough to make 1/4 cup and reserve the rest.

2. Mix 1 cup apricot syrup with the pineapple juice and heat to boiling point.

3. Soften the gelatine for 5 minutes in the water. Then dissolve it in the hot fruit juice.

4. Add the chopped apricots to half the gelatine and pour into a small ring mold. Refrigerate until set.

5. Chill the remaining gelatine until it begins to thicken.

6. Blend the cream cheese with the cream, add green pepper, paprika and salt, and spread on top of the firm gelatine.

7. Cover with the remaining thickened gelatine and set aside until firm.

8. Unmold and fill the center with watercress or lettuce and the remaining apricots.

Molded Grapefruit Salad

To serve with chicken, ham or veal (Serves 4)

1 can (about 16 oz) grapefruit
2 envelopes unflavored gelatine
2 tablespoons lemon juice
1 dessert apple, peeled, cored and
   chopped
2–3 stalks celery, chopped
lettuce

1. Drain the syrup from the grapefruit, and add sufficient water to make 1 cup.

2. Soften the gelatine in a little of the syrup for 5–10 minutes. Then stir over hot water until melted. Add the rest of the syrup and lemon juice, and leave in a cold place until it begins to thicken.

3. Stir in the grapefruit, apple and celery. Pour into a prepared mold or into individual molds, and refrigerate until set.

4. Serve on a bed of lettuce.

Jellied Tomato and Apple

A colorful accompaniment to any cold meat or poultry (Serves 4)

1 envelope unflavored gelatine
1/2 cup water
1.1/2 tomato juice
1 tablespoon Worcestershire sauce
seasoning
1 large apple, peeled, cored and chopped
1/4 cup chopped cooked ham
lettuce

1. Soften the gelatine in the water for 5—10 minutes.

2. Put it into a pan with the tomato juice and melt over low heat.

3. Remove from the heat, add Worcestershire sauce and seasoning and set aside until it begins to thicken.

4. Add apple and ham, adjust the seasoning and pour into 4 prepared individual molds.

5. Refrigerate until set, then serve on a bed of lettuce.

Jellied Tongue and Potato Salad

When this salad is unmolded, the meat is on the top and the vegetables form the base (Serves 6)

1.1/2 envelopes unflavored gelatine
1/4 cup cold water
1.1/2 cups stock
1/4 teaspoon dry mustard
a pinch of cayenne pepper
1 teaspoon Worcestershire sauce
1.1/2 cups diced cooked tongue
1.1/2 cups diced cooked potato
1/2 cup diced celery
1/4 diced green pepper
1/4 cup mayonnaise (see p. 24)
2 tablespoons vinegar
1/2 teaspoon salt
1/8 teaspoon pepper

1. Soften the gelatine in the cold water for about 10 minutes. Add boiling stock, stir until the gelatine has melted, then divide in half and leave to cool.

2. Mix the mustard and cayenne smoothly with the Worcestershire sauce and add to one half of the melted gelatine.

3. Put the tongue into the bottom of a plain mold or loaf pan rinsed out with cold water and pour the seasoned gelatine on top. Refrigerate until set.

4. Combine all the other ingredients with the rest of the gelatine and when the meat layer is set, pour it on top.

5. Leave until set. Then unmold and garnish as desired.

DRESSINGS

Salad Cream

This salad cream will keep well in the refrigerator (Makes about 12 fl. oz)

2 eggs
2 teaspoons sugar
1 tablespoon butter
1 cup milk
3/4 cup vinegar
1 teaspoon salt
a small pinch of cayenne pepper
1 teaspoon dry mustard
2 teaspoons cornstarch

1. Separate the eggs and put the yolks, sugar, butter, 2/3 of the milk, vinegar and seasonings into the top of a double boiler. Stir over boiling water until the ingredients are well blended.

2. Blend the cornstarch with the remaining milk, add to the other ingredients and stir until the mixture thickens.

3. When cold, fold in the stiffly beaten egg whites.

Green Sauce

For seafood or green salads (Makes about 8 fl. oz)

1 slice white bread
1/2 cup water
1 cup parsley
1/4 cup drained capers
4 anchovy fillets
2 cloves garlic
2 tablespoons chopped onion
1 small gherkin
1/2 cup olive oil
1/2 teaspoon salt
1/4 teaspoon freshly ground black
  pepper
1 tablespoon white wine vinegar

1. Soak the bread in the water, drain, and mash smooth.

2. Put all except the last four ingredients into a blender and blend into a paste. If a blender is not available, chop the ingredients very finely, or put through a mincer, and work into a paste.

3. Turn the mixture into a bowl and work in 2 teaspoons of the oil, salt and pepper. Then add the remaining oil gradually, stirring all the time until the mixture is smooth.

4. Stir in the vinegar and adjust the seasoning to taste.

Herb Dressing

1 clove garlic, crushed
1 tablespoon each finely chopped
  parsley, tarragon, chervil and chives
8 tablespoons olive oil
3 tablespoons white wine vinegar
salt, freshly ground black pepper

Combine garlic and herbs with oil and vinegar. Add salt and pepper to taste.

Mayonnaise

2 egg yolks
1/2 teaspoon salt
1/4 teaspoon dry mustard
1.1/2 teaspoons wine vinegar
1 cup olive oil
1/2 teaspoon lemon juice

1. Rinse a bowl with hot water and dry well.

2. Put in the egg yolks, salt and mustard and 1 teaspoon of the vinegar. Beat vigorously or at low speed with an electric mixer.

3. Add half the oil, drop by drop, and then the remaining vinegar.

4. Beat in the rest of the oil in a steady stream.

5. Add lemon juice.

Note
If the mayonnaise curdles, break an egg yolk into a clean basin and gradually beat the curdled mixture into it.

Cooked Mayonnaise

2 tablespoons wine vinegar
2 tablespoons water
2 tablespoons sugar
1 tablespoon butter
1/2 teaspoon salt
1 teaspoon dry mustard
1 beaten egg

1. Combine all the ingredients in a saucepan. Stir over a low heat until the butter melts and the mixture thickens slightly.

2. Remove from the heat and chill.

Chiffonade Dressing

1 cup French dressing (see p. 26)
1 hard-boiled egg, chopped
1 teaspoon finely chopped parsley
1 tablespoon finely chopped pimento
1 teaspoon finely chopped chives
1/8 teaspoon paprika

For vegetable salads

Combine all ingredients.

Cottage Cheese Dressing

1 cup French dressing (see p. 26)
3 tablespoons cottage cheese
2 tablespoons chopped parsley
1 tablespoon finely chopped
  chutney

For fruit, vegetable or green salads

Combine all ingredients and chill before serving.

Cucumber Cream Dressing

2 tablespoons vinegar
2 tablespoons sugar
1 cup peeled, diced cucumber
1 cup whipped cream

For meat or chicken salads

Mix the vinegar, sugar and cucumber and fold into the whipped cream.

Aïoli

This garlic sauce is very popular in France. Serve with fish, potato salad or boiled beef (Makes about 1.1/4 cups)

1 slice French bread
milk
3 cloves garlic, crushed very finely
2 egg yolks
1/8 teaspoon salt
8 fl. oz olive oil
1/2 teaspoon cold water
1 teaspoon lemon juice

1. Remove crust from the bread, and discard it. Soak bread in a little milk, then squeeze it out.

2. Add garlic, egg yolks and salt, and beat well.

3. Add oil very slowly as for mayonnaise and, as the dressing thickens, beat in the water and lemon juice.

Cream Dressing

To serve with lettuce (Makes about 8 fl. oz)

1/2 teaspoon prepared mustard
1 teaspoon sugar
2 teaspoons tarragon vinegar
1/2 clove garlic, crushed
1 hard-boiled egg
1 teaspoon chopped tarragon or chives
1/2 cup light cream

1. Mix the mustard, sugar and vinegar together, add the garlic and yolk of the hard-boiled egg. Mix well, then stir in cream and chopped tarragon or chives. If the vinegar makes the cream too thick for pouring, add a few drops of water or milk.

2. Chill thoroughly, then pour over crisp lettuce hearts and sprinkle with the chopped egg white.

French Dressing

2 tablespoons white wine vinegar
salt
freshly ground black pepper
6—8 tablespoons olive oil

Mix vinegar with salt and pepper to taste. Add oil and beat with a fork until the mixture thickens.

Note
For a slightly thicker dressing, add a cube of ice and stir for 1—2 minutes longer, then remove the ice cube.

VARIATIONS

TARRAGON DRESSING
Add 1 teaspoon chopped fresh tarragon leaves.

CURRY DRESSING
Add 1/2 teaspoon curry powder and 1 teaspoon finely chopped shallots.

CAPER DRESSING
Add 1 teaspoon chopped capers, 1/2 clove garlic, finely crushed, and a little anchovy paste.

ROQUEFORT DRESSING
Add 3 tablespoons crumbled Roquefort cheese and blend well. Chill before serving.

Russian Dressing

1 cup mayonnaise (see p. 24)
1 tablespoon chili sauce
1—2 teaspoons chopped chives
2 teaspoons chopped red pepper or
  canned pimento

For egg or vegetable salads or with fish (Makes about 8 fl. oz)

Combine all ingredients.

Note
Chili sauce varies considerably in strength. It is advisable to add about 1/2 teaspoon, then taste and increase the quantity as necessary. The quantity given is for a mild chili sauce.

Green Goddess Dressing

1 cup mayonnaise (see p. 24)
1 clove garlic, crushed
1/4 cup finely chopped parsley
2 tablespoons chopped chives
1 tablespoon lemon juice
1 tablespoon tarragon vinegar
1/2 teaspoon salt, black pepper
2 teaspoons anchovy paste
2 tablespoons cream

For all seafood salads (Makes about 2 cups)

Combine all ingredients and stir until dressing is smooth.

Thousand Island Dressing

1 cup mayonnaise (see p. 24)
1 tablespoon chili sauce (see note
  above)
1 tablespoon chopped green olives
2 teaspoons finely chopped chives

For meat or fish salads (Makes about 1 cup)

Combine all ingredients.

Dressings (see p. 26)

Fruit Salad Dressing

(Makes about 1.3/4 cups)

1/4 cup current jelly
1 cup mayonnaise (see p. 24)
1/2 cup sour cream
1/4 cup chopped toasted almonds

1. Melt the jelly and leave to get cold.

2. Combine with the other ingredients and chill before using.

FRUIT SALADS

Stuffed Pears

Fresh pears stuffed with crab meat, apple and celery. Very good served with cold pork or poultry or as an hors d'oeuvre (Serves 6)

3 large ripe pears
lemon juice
2 red skinned dessert apples, cored and diced but not peeled
2–3 stalks celery, diced
1 can crab meat
1 tablespoon finely chopped onion
1 tablespoon chopped parsley
French dressing (see p. 26)
lettuce

1. Wipe the pears but do not peel them. Cut in halves, remove the cores and scoop out some of the flesh. Brush the pear halves with lemon juice.

2. Put the scooped-out flesh into a bowl and add apple, celery, crab meat, onion and parsley. Add enough French dressing to moisten, mix well and check the seasoning.

3. Spoon into the pear halves, arrange on a bed of lettuce and garnish with thin slices of unpeeled apple brushed with lemon juice.

Honeyed Salad

To serve with cold turkey or galantines (Serves 4–5)

4 dessert apples
1/2 cup seeded or seedless raisins
1/4 cup chopped walnuts
1.1/2 cups cooked, diced carrots
a pinch of salt

DRESSING
1 tablespoon clear honey
3 tablespoons lemon juice

1. Peel, core and dice three of the apples and combine with the raisins, nuts and carrots. Add a pinch of salt.

2. Add the honey and lemon juice blended together, toss lightly and set aside in a cool place for about 1 hour.

3. Arrange in a salad bowl or on a platter and garnish with the remaining apple—unpeeled, cut into slices and brushed with lemon juice.

Frozen Fruit Salad

1 package (3 oz) cream cheese
3 tablespoons mayonnaise (see p. 24)
a pinch of salt
1 cup whipped cream
1/4 cup chopped dates (seeded)
1/4 cup maraschino cherries
1/4 cup crushed pineapple
1/4 cup chopped kumquats
    (seeded)
1 tablespoon finely chopped preserved
    ginger
1/2 cup chopped blanched almonds
lettuce

A delicious mixture of fruit and cream cheese, folded into whipped cream and frozen (Serves 6—8)

1. Blend the cheese and mayonnaise, add a pinch of salt and fold in the whipped cream, fruits and ginger.

2. Pour into refrigerator trays, sprinkle with almonds and freeze until firm.

3. Cut into squares and serve on lettuce.

Pear and Grape Salad

This exciting looking salad is delicious served with cold ham or pork
(Serves 4)

1. Peel the pears, cut in half and scoop out the core with a teaspoon.

2. Blend the cream cheese with enough French dressing to make it spreadable and coat the rounded side of each pear half.

3. Halve and seed the grapes and press them into the cheese, close together so that each pear half resembles a small bunch of grapes.

4. Serve on crisp lettuce leaves.

4 ripe dessert pears
1 cup cream cheese
1—2 tablespoons French dressing
   (see p. 26)
1/2 lb black grapes
crisp lettuce

Brandied Fruit Salad

A simple but delicious fruit salad for a special occasion dessert
(Serves 5—6)

1. Combine all the fruit, sprinkle with sugar. Mix the brandy and wine and pour over the fruit.

2. Mix lightly but thoroughly and chill for at least 3 hours to blend the flavors.

3 apples, peeled, cored and thinly
   sliced
3 pears, peeled, cored and sliced
2 oranges, peeled, all white pith
   removed, then sliced
1 cup melon balls, fresh or frozen
1 cup seeded cherries
1/2 cup sugar
1/4 cup brandy
1.1/4 cups white wine

Pear and Cheese Salad

A very good flavor combination is obtained by stuffing pears with Gorgonzola cheese (Serves 3)

3 large ripe pears
4 oz Gorgonzola cheese
2—3 tablespoons whipped cream
seasoning
curly endive or lettuce
paprika pepper

1. Peel, halve and core the pears.

2. Combine the cheese, whipped cream and a little seasoning and beat until smooth and creamy.

3. Put into a pastry bag with a rose nozzle and pipe some cheese mixture into the center of the pears. Press the two halves together, and pipe the remaining cheese where the pears join.

4. Arrange on a bed of endive or lettuce and sprinkle lightly with paprika.

Waldorf Salad

A good winter salad of fruit and nuts combined with mayonnaise and sour cream (Serves 3—4)

1/2 cup mayonnaise (see p. 24)
1/2 cup sour cream
1 tablespoon honey
1.1/2 cups tart apples, peeled, cored
    and diced
1 cup diced celery
1/2 cup coarsely chopped walnuts
1 cup halved, seeded grapes

1. Combine mayonnaise, sour cream and honey.

2. Add apple and mix well to prevent the apple discoloring.

3. Add celery, walnuts and grapes. Mix again lightly and chill well before serving.

VARIATION
Substitute diced pears for the apple or use half of each—or add 1 sliced banana with the apple.

Lettuce and Orange Salad

Especially good served with chicken, and for those who dislike an oily dressing (Serves 4)

2 oranges
1 iceberg lettuce
sugar
1/4 cup roasted and salted almonds

DRESSING
2 tablespoons butter
1/4 clove garlic, crushed very finely
teaspoon lemon juice

1. Cut the oranges in half lengthways, and each half into four pieces. Remove the pulp with a sharp knife, remove seeds and any white pith.

2. Arrange the lettuce in a salad bowl, put the orange pieces on top, sprinkle with a little sugar and add the almonds.

3. For the dressing—melt the butter with the garlic, add lemon juice, mix well and pour into the bowl.

4. Toss the ingredients very lightly.

OMELETTES & OTHER EGG DISHES

Cheese and Ham Omelette

An omelette is perhaps the most popular dish for a snack. It is quick to prepare, light and nourishing. A 2-egg omelette is generally sufficient for 1 person, allow 4 eggs for 2–3 servings.

4 eggs
1 tablespoon water
1/2 teaspoon salt
1/4 teaspoon freshly ground black pepper
1/2 cup cooked ham, cut into fine strips
1/2 cup cottage cheese, well drained
1 tablespoon butter
1 tablespoon oil

1. Beat the eggs, water, salt and pepper until just blended. Add ham and cheese.

2. Heat the butter and oil in a 9 inch skillet. Pour in the egg mixture and cook over medium heat, stirring with a fork, for a few seconds, then lift the eggs to allow the uncooked mixture to run underneath.

3. Fold over and roll out on to a hot dish.

Californian Omelette

3 eggs
1 tablespoon milk
1 tablespoon water
1/2 teaspoon salt
1/8 teaspoon black pepper
1/4 cup diced avocado pear
3—4 tablespoons very finely chopped cooked chicken
1 tablespoon finely chopped chives
1 tablespoon butter
1 tablespoon oil
1 tablespoon cream

(Serves 2)

1. Beat the eggs lightly, add milk, water, seasoning, avocado, chicken and chives.

2. Heat the butter and oil in a skillet, pour in the egg mixture, stir lightly with a fork until the mixture just begins to set.

3. Pour on the cream, cook a minute longer then fold over and serve at once.

Chicken Liver Omelette

FILLING
3 tablespoons butter
2 tablespoons minced onion
1/4 cup chopped mushrooms
1/4 lb chicken livers
1 tablespoon flour
3/4 cup chicken stock
1 teaspoon tomato paste
1/8 teaspoon thyme

OMELETTE
4 eggs
1/4 teaspoon salt
1/8 teaspoon black pepper
2 tablespoons cold water
1 tablespoon butter

(Serves 2–3)

1. Heat the butter in a skillet, sauté the onion, mushrooms and chicken livers until the livers are browned, then remove them from the pan and keep hot.

2. Add the flour to the skillet and mix with the pan juices. Add the stock and stir until boiling. Add tomato paste, seasoning and thyme and cook for 5 minutes.

3. Return the livers to the pan and re-heat.

4. Prepare the omelette in the usual way and spread with the liver mixture just before serving.

Tomato Omelette

FILLING
2 tablespoons olive oil
4 tablespoons minced onion
1/8 teaspoon minced garlic
1.1/2 cups peeled, seeded and chopped
    tomatoes
1/2 teaspoon salt
1/4 teaspoon black pepper
1 tablespoon chopped parsley

OMELETTE
4 eggs
1/4 teaspoon salt
1/8 teaspoon pepper
2 tablespoons cold water
1 tablespoon butter

(Serves 2–3)

1. Heat the oil in a skillet, sauté the onion and garlic for 5 minutes. Stir in tomatoes, salt and pepper and cook over low heat until the tomato is soft. Then add parsley.

2. Prepare the omelette in the usual way. When the eggs are just set, put the tomato mixture in the centre and fold over.

3. Turn out on to a hot dish and serve at once.

Devilled Omelette

3 eggs
cayenne pepper
1/4 teaspoon dry mustard
a pinch of curry powder
2 tablespoons water
2 tablespoons light cream
1/4 cup chopped cooked ham
1 tablespoon butter

(Serves 2–3)

1. Beat the eggs lightly, add seasoning, mustard and curry powder. Stir in water, cream and chopped ham.

2. Heat the butter in a small skillet, pour in the egg mixture and cook quickly, stirring occasionally with a fork and loosening the omelette from the side of the pan.

3. When the omelette is lightly set on the under side, put the skillet under a hot broiler to brown the top.

4. Fold over and serve at once.

Cottage Eggs

6 eggs
1/2 teaspoon salt
1/4 teaspoon pepper
2 tablespoons light cream
1/2 cup cottage cheese
2 tablespoons butter
4–5 slices hot buttered toast

(Serves 4–5)

1. Beat the eggs lightly, season with salt and pepper.

2. Blend the cream with the cottage cheese and stir in the eggs.

3. Heat the butter in a skillet, pour in the egg mixture and cook lightly as for scrambled eggs.

4. Serve on hot toast.

Scrambled Eggs with Oysters

Canned oysters are excellent for this unusual snack (Serves 4)

6 eggs
dash of Tabasco
2 tablespoons butter
1 teaspoon anchovy paste
1 can oysters
freshly ground black pepper
1 tablespoon finely chopped parsley
croûtons of fried bread

1. Whisk the eggs very lightly with the Tabasco (avoid over-beating).

2. Put the butter and anchovy paste into a small skillet and when hot pour in the eggs. Stir until just beginning to set, then add the oysters, drained and chopped. Season with salt and black pepper.

3. Finish scrambling the eggs but avoid over-cooking.

4. Put on to hot serving dishes, sprinkle with parsley and serve with croûtons of fried bread or with toast.

Fried Eggs Romano

Eggs fried with bacon and green peppers (Serves 4)

2 tablespoons olive oil
1 onion, peeled and thinly sliced
1 green pepper, seeded and cut into
    strips
4 slices bacon, cut into pieces
4 eggs

1. Heat the oil in a sauté pan, add onion, green pepper and bacon, and cook over medium heat until the onion is transparent.

2. Break the eggs into the pan carefully, cover with the lid of the pan or with foil and continue to cook for 2—3 minutes or until the eggs are just firm. Add a dash of salt and pepper if desired.

3. Slide carefully on to a hot serving dish.

Eggs Valencia

2 green peppers, seeded and
    chopped
1/2 cup light cream
1/2 teaspoon salt
3 teaspoons Tabasco
4 eggs
1/2 cup grated Parmesan cheese

Pre-heat oven to 375°F

Eggs cooked in a blend of cream and green pepper with cheese (Serves 4)

1. Blend the peppers and cream in an electric mixer, add salt and Tabasco and pour into a buttered ovenproof baking pan.

2. Break each egg carefully on top, sprinkle with the cheese and cook in a moderate oven until the eggs are set—about 10 minutes.

Bacon Omelette

(Serves 2—3)

3 tablespoons butter
4 scallions, sliced
4 eggs
2 tablespoons whipping cream
1/2 teaspoon salt
1/4 teaspoon pepper
1 teaspoon prepared mustard
6 slices crisply fried bacon

1. Melt half the butter in a skillet and sauté the onion for 3 minutes. Then remove from the pan.

2. Beat the eggs, cream, salt, pepper and mustard until the mixture is just blended. Add the onion and bacon.

3. Heat the remaining butter in the skillet, pour in the egg mixture and cook over low heat, stirring lightly with a fork and lifting the eggs to allow the uncooked mixture to run underneath.

4. When the eggs are just set, fold over and turn out on to a hot dish.

Piperade

An appetizing mixture of eggs and vegetables, originating from the Basque region of France (Serves 4)

3 tablespoons olive oil
1 green pepper, seeded and thinly
　sliced
1 onion, peeled and finely chopped
1 tomato, peeled, seeded and chopped
1 clove garlic, crushed
1 teaspoon salt
1/8 teaspoon freshly ground black
　pepper
6 eggs

1. Heat the oil in a skillet, add the green pepper and onion, and sauté until the vegetables begin to soften.

2. Add tomato, garlic and seasoning, and simmer until the ingredients are soft and mushy.

3. Add the lightly beaten eggs and stir just enough to mix with the vegetables. Cook for a few minutes until the eggs are just set.

4. Serve with toast or on thin sautéd slices of ham.

Eggs in Snow

An attractive variation of the simplest of all snacks—eggs on toast (Serves 2)

1. Toast the bread on one side, turn and toast the under side very lightly. Butter the lightly toasted side and keep hot.

2. Separate the eggs, add seasoning and a pinch of nutmeg to the egg whites, and beat until stiff.

2 slices bread
butter
2 eggs
nutmeg
grated cheese

3. Spread the egg white over the buttered toast, make a slight indentation in the middle and drop in the egg yolk.

4. Sprinkle with grated cheese and put under a hot broiler for a few minutes until the egg yolk has set.

Golden Buck

A tasty mixture of eggs and cheese served on toast (Serves 4)

2 tablespoons butter
1.1/2 cups grated cheese
4 tablespoons beer or ale
1 teaspoon Worcestershire sauce
1 teaspoon lemon juice
cayenne pepper
a pinch of celery salt
4 eggs
4 slices buttered toast

1. Melt the butter in a small skillet, add cheese, beer, Worcestershire sauce, lemon juice and seasoning. Stir over low heat until smooth and creamy.

2. Beat the eggs lightly and stir into the mixture. Stir until the eggs are lightly set, then spoon on to the hot toast.

Scotch Woodcock

A simple snack of scrambled eggs with anchovies (Serves 4)

1/4 cup butter
4 slices of bread
anchovy paste
6 eggs
8 anchovy filets
capers
cayenne pepper

1. Heat half the butter in a pan and fry the bread until crisp. Remove from pan, spread very lightly with anchovy paste and keep hot.

2. Put the rest of the butter into the pan, add the eggs, beaten very slightly with pepper and a small pinch of salt. Stir until just set.

3. Spoon the scrambled egg on to the fried bread and arrange 2 anchovy filets across each piece. Put a caper into each section, sprinkle sparingly with cayenne and serve at once.

Bacon and Kidney Scramble

Kidney, bacon and eggs cooked together and served on toast (Serves 4)

2 lamb   kidneys
3—4 tablespoons butter
4 slices bacon
3 eggs
1 tablespoon cream
black pepper
a pinch of mixed herbs
4 slices hot buttered toast

1. Skin the kidneys, remove the cores and cut into thin slices.

2. Heat the butter in a small skillet, add kidney, fry for a few minutes, then add the chopped bacon and cook together until the kidney is tender.

3. Beat the eggs lightly, add cream, seasoning and herbs and pour over the kidneys. Stir over low heat until the eggs are lightly set.

4. Serve on hot buttered toast.

Egg and Corn Savoury

Eggs covered with sweetcorn in a cheese sauce and lightly grilled (Serves 4)

4 eggs
1 can (12 oz) corn
milk
1/4 cup butter
3 tablespoons flour
cayenne pepper
1 cup grated cheese
2 tablespoons breadcrumbs
a little extra butter

1. Boil the eggs for 5 minutes.

2. Drain the corn, measure the liquid and add sufficient milk to make 1.1/2 cups.

3. Make a sauce with the butter, flour, milk and corn liquor. Add seasoning, most of the cheese, and corn.

4. Put half this sauce into a buttered baking dish. Shell the eggs and arrange on top. Cover with the remaining sauce.

5. Mix the remaining cheese with breadcrumbs, sprinkle on top and dot with butter.

6. Brown under a hot broiler.

Swiss Eggs

A light but nourishing snack of eggs and cheese with cream (Serves 6)

6 eggs
1 cup grated cheese
1/2 cup cream
1 teaspoon finely chopped parsley
2 tablespoons butter

Pre-heat oven to 375°F

1. Break the eggs carefully into a buttered ovenproof dish and sprinkle with salt and pepper. Cover with half the cheese.

2. Pour the cream on top and sprinkle with the remaining cheese and parsley.

3. Dot with butter and put into a moderately hot oven until the eggs are just set—about 7 to 10 minutes.

CHEESE DISHES & FONDUES

Welsh Rarebit

The Welsh Rarebit available in cans is very good, but if you prefer to make your own it takes only a few minutes. In this recipe the cheese is melted in ale or beer and the curry powder adds piquancy to the flavor (Serves 4)

1 cup ale or beer
2 teaspoons Worcestershire sauce
1/4 teaspoon dry mustard
1/4 teaspoon curry powder
a small pinch cayenne pepper
4 cups grated sharp Cheddar cheese
4 slices toast or English muffins or
   broiled tomatoes

1. Combine the beer, Worcestershire sauce, mustard, curry powder and cayenne pepper in a skillet or chafing dish. Cook over low heat until the ingredients are well mixed and hot.

2. Add the cheese and stir until melted. Serve at once on hot buttered toast or toasted English muffins or it is very good served on hot broiled tomatoes.

Puffed Cheese Rarebit

(Serves 4)

4 slices bread
butter
3 eggs
1 cup grated cheese
1/4 teaspoon prepared mustard
1—2 tablespoons cream

Pre-heat oven to 400°F

1. Toast the bread, spread with butter and arrange the slices in an ovenproof dish.

2. Separate the eggs, beat the yolks, add cheese, mustard, seasoning and cream.

3. Beat the egg whites stiffly and fold into the mixture. Pile onto the slices of toast and put into a moderately hot oven for about 7 minutes or until brown and puffy.

Mushroom Rarebit

A variation of Welsh Rarebit, another good way of serving mushrooms as a snack (Serves 4)

1/4 cup butter
4 cups sliced mushrooms
2 tablespoons tomato purée
3 tablespoons stock or water
4 tablespoons grated Parmesan cheese
4 slices toast or English muffins

1. Heat the butter in a pan, add the mushrooms and sauté slowly for about 10 minutes.

2. Add seasoning and tomato purée mixed with the stock. Add cheese and continue to cook slowly until the mushrooms are tender—about 5 to 7 minutes.

3. Serve on hot buttered toast or English muffins.

Cheese Puff

A light and airy cheese spread for toast or muffins

2 egg whites
1/2 teaspoon baking powder
1/4 teaspoon salt
1/4 teaspoon paprika
1 cup grated sharp Cheddar cheese
4 slices hot buttered toast

1. Beat the egg whites until stiff. Stir in the baking powder and salt sifted together. Add paprika and grated cheese and fold in lightly.

2. Spread on the toast about 1/4 inch thick and brown under a hot broiler. Serve at once.

Cheese and Ham Toast

(Serves 4)

4 slices cooked ham
4 slices buttered toast
a little chopped chutney
4 slices Gruyère cheese
2 tomatoes, peeled and sliced

1. Put a slice of ham on each piece of toast. Spread lightly with chutney and cover with a slice of cheese.

2. Arrange slices of tomato on top and put under a hot broiler to heat through.

Cheese and Bacon Slices

2 cups grated cheese
1 egg
1 teaspoon Worcestershire sauce
1/8 teaspoon prepared mustard
cayenne pepper
1 tablespoon butter
4 slices bread
4 slices bacon
4 black olives

Pre-heat oven to 400°F

(Serves 4)

1. Combine the cheese with beaten egg, Worcestershire sauce and seasonings. Spread on the bread and top with a slice of bacon.

2. Put into a buttered baking pan and bake in a moderately hot oven for 10 minutes.

3. Place an olive on top and serve at once.

Turkey Gratin

Slices of turkey or chicken on toast covered with a piquant cheese sauce (Serves 4)

1.1/2 tablespoons butter
1.1/2 tablespoons flour
1/4 teaspoon dry mustard
1 cup milk
3 cups grated cheese
1 teaspoon Worcestershire sauce
4 slices toast
8 fairly thick slices turkey
paprika

1. Heat the butter, stir in the flour and mustard. Cook for 2 minutes. Then add the milk gradually and stir until boiling. Add salt and pepper to taste.

2. Add cheese and Worcestershire sauce and stir over low heat until the cheese has melted.

3. Arrange the toast in a shallow baking pan, put the slices of turkey on top and cover with the cheese sauce.

4. Brown under a hot broiler and sprinkle with paprika before serving.

Cheese and Anchovy Snack

A hot snack composed of slices of bread and melted cheese topped with anchovy. If you find anchovies a little too salty to your taste, soak them for 10—15 minutes in a little milk and then pat dry before using (Serves 4)

1/4 French loaf
Bel Paese or Cheddar cheese
1 can anchovy filets
1/2 cup butter

Pre-heat oven to 400°F

1. Cut the bread into slanting slices about 1/4 inch thick. Place a slice of cheese on each and arrange in a baking pan, slightly overlapping. Put into a moderately hot oven until the cheese has melted and the bread is crisp.

2. Mash the anchovy filets and mix with the butter. Spread over the bread and return to the oven for a few minutes to heat through.

Mexican Cheese

Served on toast, this appetizing mixture of cheese, tomatoes and eggs makes a good snack. For a more substantial dish, try it on cooked rice (Serves 4—5)

2 tablespoons oil
1 green pepper, seeded and chopped
1 /2 cup finely chopped onion
1 tablespoon flour
1/2 cup milk
3 cups grated American cheese
1 cup drained, canned tomatoes
1 canned pimento, cut into strips
3 tablespoons chopped black olives,
cayenne pepper
3 egg yolks
toast or cooked rice

1. Heat the oil in a pan, add the green pepper and onion and sauté for about 10 minutes.

2. Stir in the flour and milk and stir until boiling.

3. Add cheese and tomatoes and cook over low heat for about 10 minutes. Add pimento, olives and seasoning and cook another few minutes.

4. Add the beaten egg yolks gradually and stir with a fork until the mixture thickens. It should not boil at this stage.

5. Serve on toast or with cooked rice.

Swiss Fondue

This recipe is for the traditional Neuchâtel fondue (Serves 4)

1 clove garlic
1.1/2 cups dry white wine
1 teaspoon lemon juice
3 cups grated Emmenthal cheese
3 cups grated Gruyère cheese
2 teaspoons cornstarch
2 tablespoons Kirsch
white pepper
cayenne pepper
grated nutmeg
paprika

1. Rub the inside of the fondue pot with the cut clove of garlic.

2. Put in the wine and lemon juice, and heat over a low flame. Add the cheese gradually, stirring all the time using a figure of eight motion.

3. When the mixture bubbles add the cornstarch, blended smoothly with the Kirsch, and cook for about 3 minutes. Add pepper, cayenne, nutmeg and paprika to taste.

4. To serve, spear a piece of bread on to the fondue fork and dip into the fondue. If the crust is left on the bread it is easier to spear and it is advisable not to have the bread too fresh, or it will crumble in the fondue.

Tomato Fondue with Frankfurters

French bread is served separately with this fondue, and small frankfurters are used for dipping (Serves 2—3)

1 clove garlic
2 cups grated Cheddar or American cheese
1/2 cup grated Gruyère cheese
1/2 cup condensed tomato soup
1 teaspoon Worcestershire sauce
3 tablespoons dry sherry
1 small can cocktail frankfurters
French bread

1. Rub the inside of the fondue pot with the cut clove of garlic.

2. Put in the cheeses, tomato soup and Worcestershire sauce, and stir continuously over a low heat until the cheese has melted and the mixture is creamy. Stir in the sherry, and cook 2—3 minutes. Adjust the seasoning before serving.

3. The frankfurters are then speared on to the fondue forks and dipped into the fondue.

4. Serve with plenty of French bread.

English Style Fondue

Beer or ale is used in this recipe instead of wine (Serves 3—4)

1 cup beer or ale
2 cups grated Cheddar cheese
1 clove garlic, crushed
2 tablespoons butter
2 tablespoons cornstarch
1/2 teaspoon dry mustard
a little extra beer or ale

1. Put the beer, cheese and crushed garlic into the fondue pot and stir over low heat until the cheese has melted.

2. Stir in the butter.

3. Blend the cornstarch and mustard smoothly with a little extra beer and stir into the fondue. Continue stirring until the mixture is thick and creamy.

FRIED & TOASTED SANDWICHES & SANDWICH SPREADS

Monte Cristo Sandwich

A crisp fried sandwich of chicken or turkey, ham and cheese (Serves 4)

8 slices bread
2 eggs
1/2 cup milk
1/2 teaspoon salt
a pinch of pepper
sliced breast of chicken or turkey
4 slices cooked ham
4 slices Swiss cheese
prepared mustard
butter for frying

1. Cut the crusts from the bread.

2. Beat the eggs, milk, salt and pepper together. Dip the slices of bread in the mixture and allow them to soak well, then drain.

3. Arrange some thin slices of chicken on 4 of the slices of bread. Cover with a slice of ham and top with a slice of cheese. Spread lightly with mustard and cover each with another slice of bread. Press down well and cut across diagonally.

4. Heat the butter in a skillet and fry the sandwiches until brown and crisp, turning once. Serve while hot.

Cheese Fingers

9 slices bread
butter
1/2 cup grated cheese
2 eggs
2 tablespoons milk
butter for frying

1. Remove the crusts from the bread, spread with butter and make into sandwiches with the grated cheese. (Spread a little prepared mustard or chopped pickle on one side of the bread if desired.)

2. Cut into neat fingers.

3. Beat the eggs, add milk and seasoning.

4. Dip the fingers quickly in and out of the egg and fry in hot butter until crisp and golden.

Toasted Cheese and Bacon Sandwich

A hearty snack with bacon, cheese and prunes (Serves 4)

12 prunes
8 slices bread
butter
8 slices bacon
4 slices Gouda or processed cheese
watercress for garnish

Pre-heat broiler

1. Cover the prunes with boiling water and let stand about 1 hour.

2. Remove crusts from the bread and butter one side of each slice.

3. Broil the bacon until crisp, set aside 2 slices and chop the rest coarsely.

4. Remove the seeds from the prunes, set aside 4 and chop the remainder.

5. Cover half the slices of buttered bread with the chopped prunes and bacon. Top with the remaining slices.

6. Toast the sandwiches on one side, turn over and cover the untoasted side with a slice of cheese. Broil until the cheese bubbles and browns.

7. Top each sandwich with half a slice of bacon and a prune. Serve hot garnished with watercress.

Swiss Cheese Snack

Cheese and ham sandwiches fried in butter (Serves 4)

8 slices bread
butter
prepared mustard
4 slices Swiss cheese
4 thin slices cooked ham

1. Cut the crusts from the bread and spread with butter.

2. Spread a little mustard on half the slices, put a slice of cheese and a slice of ham on top. Cover with the remaining slices of bread and press down firmly.

3. Cut in half crossways and fry in hot butter, turning once.

Chicken Club Sandwich

A club sandwich consists of 3 slices of toast for each sandwich. The filling can vary, but it is generally some kind of poultry or meat and salad. The sandwich should always be served hot (Makes 1 club sandwich)

slices bread
butter
mayonnaise (see p. 24)
lettuce
slices of chicken breast
prepared mustard
2 slices bacon, fried until crisp
1—2 slices tomato or onion
gherkins or stuffed olives for garnish

1. Remove the crusts from the bread, toast and spread with butter.

2. Spread the first slice with a little mayonnaise, cover with 1—2 leaves of lettuce and slices of chicken. Spread a little more mayonnaise on the chicken and cover with the second slice of toast.

3. Spread a very little mustard on the toast and then a little mayonnaise. Cover with the slices of bacon and slices of tomato or onion.

4. Place the third slice of toast on top and press down firmly. Serve at once, garnished with slices of gherkin or stuffed olive.

Sandwich Spreads

Below are a selection of spreads which can be made up for a quick sandwich. In most cases, the sandwiches could be fried or grilled if you prefer a hot snack.

Avocado Spread

4 oz mashed avocado
2 teaspoons ground onion
1 tablespoon lemon juice
1 tablespoon mayonnaise (see p. 24)
a pinch of cayenne pepper
a dash of Tabasco

Combine all ingredients and beat until smooth.

Cream Cheese and Orange Spread

1 package (3 oz) cream cheese
2 tablespoons finely crystallized or
    preserved ginger
2 teaspoons grated orange rind
3 tablespoons orange juice

(see picture, p. 57)

Beat the cream cheese until soft and smooth. Add ginger and orange rind and mix in the orange juice.

Blue Cheese Spread

1/4 lb blue cheese
2 packages cream cheese
2 tablespoons mayonnaise (see p. 24)
2 tablespoons crisply cooked diced
    bacon

Combine the cheeses, and blend until creamy and smooth. Add the mayonnaise and bacon.

Cheese and Pimento Spread

1 cup grated Cheddar cheese
1 canned pimento, drained and
    chopped
3—4 tablespoons mayonnaise
a pinch of paprika

Blend ingredients together to form a spreadable paste.

Ham Sandwich Loaf

Prepare this in advance for a late-night snack—perhaps after the theater. The loaf is sandwiched with a variety of fillings and needs to be refrigerated for 3—4 hours (Serves 7—8, see picture p. 51)

1 loaf uncut bread
1/2 lb cooked ham, chopped
1 can (about 3.1/2 oz) pimentos,
    drained and chopped
mayonnaise (see p. 24)
1 cup sweet pickle
2 hard-boiled eggs
butter
1—1.1/2 cups cream cheese

1. Remove all crusts from the loaf and cut lengthways into 4 slices of equal thickness.

2. Combine ham and pimentos, and add enough mayonnaise to make a spreadable paste. Chop the pickle and eggs together and moisten with mayonnaise.

3. Spread one slice of bread with butter, then with half the ham mixture. Butter both sides of the second slice of bread and press over the first slice. Spread with the egg and pickle mixture.

4. Butter both sides of the third slice of bread, press on top of the egg and pickle and spread with the remaining ham and pimento mixture.

5. Butter the bottom of the top slice and press into position.

6. Place the re-shaped loaf on to a serving platter and spread the top and sides with a thick layer of cream cheese. If this does not spread easily, soften it with a little cream or milk. Refrigerate for 3—4 hours and when required cut through in slices.

SNACKS ON TOAST

Turkish Sandwich

1 tablespoon butter
1 tablespoon flour
1/2 cup chicken stock
1/4 cup light cream
1 cup cooked diced chicken
1/4 cup chopped walnuts
1 teaspoon onion juice
paprika
3 slices hot toast
butter
stuffed olives for garnish

This is an open sandwich of chicken and nuts (Serves 3)

1. Make a sauce with the butter, flour and stock, add cream, chicken and nuts, and season carefully with the onion juice, salt, pepper and paprika.

2. Heat and then pile on to the slices of toast. Brush over with a little melted butter and garnish with rings of stuffed olives. Serve at once.

Sweet – Sour Tuna Snack

4 slices bread
butter
1 can tuna fish (about 7 oz)
2–3 tablespoons mayonnaise (see p. 24)
4 slices drained canned pineapple
4 slices Cheddar or Swiss cheese

Pre-heat broiler

An interesting mixture of tuna fish, pineapple and cheese, served hot on toast (Serves 4)

1. Toast the bread on one side only and lightly butter the untoasted side.

2. Drain and flake the tuna, and add enough mayonnaise to make it spreadable. Spread on the buttered side of the toast, cover with a slice of pineapple and top with a slice of cheese.

3. Put under a hot broiler until the cheese has melted.

Cheese and Tomato Sandwich

3/4 cup grated cheese
2 tablespoons softened butter
1 teaspoon prepared mustard
1 teaspoon Worcestershire sauce
2 tomatoes
4 slices buttered toast
4 slices bacon

Pre-heat oven to 475°F

A savory mixture of cheese, tomato and bacon on toast, browned in the oven (Serves 4)

1. Combine the cheese, butter, mustard and Worcestershire sauce.

2. Peel the tomatoes, cut across in halves and then cut each half through again, making 8 slices. Place 2 slices on each slice of bread and sprinkle with salt and pepper. Cover with the cheese mixture and top with a slice of bacon.

3. Arrange on a baking tray and cook in a fairly hot oven for 5 to 7 minutes, or until the bacon is crisp and the cheese has melted.

Crabmeat Nippies

A snack of crabmeat and cheese made in minutes (Serves 4)

4 slices bread
butter
1 can (about 6 oz) crab meat
2 teaspoons mayonnaise (see p. 24)
1 teaspoon grated onion
1/2 cup grated Cheddar or American cheese

Pre-heat broiler

1. Remove the crusts from the bread and toast on one side only. Lightly butter the untoasted side.
2. Flake the crab meat, combine with the mayonnaise and onion, and spread on the buttered side of the toast. Sprinkle generously with cheese.
3. Put under a hot broiler for 1–2 minutes until the cheese melts and is lightly browned. Serve at once.

Cream Cheese & Orange Spread and Ham Sandwich Loaf (see pp. 48 & 9)

Haddock Kedgeree

(Serves 5—6)

1/4 cup butter
1 lb cooked smoked haddock, flaked
2 cups cooked rice
3 hard-boiled eggs
lemon juice
5—6 slices hot buttered toast

1. Melt the butter in a pan, add the flaked fish, and sauté for 2—3 minutes. Add the rice, 2 of the eggs, chopped, salt as desired, pepper and a good squeeze of lemon juice. Stir over the heat for a few minutes.

2. Arrange on hot toast, slice the remaining egg and use for garnish.

Clam Savory

A savory snack of clams, grated cheese, green pepper and tomato
(Serves 4—5)

3 tablespoons butter
1 small onion, peeled and finely chopped
1/2 green pepper, finely chopped
1 can (7.1/2 oz) clams drained and chopped
1 cup grated cheese
1 tablespoon tomato purée
1 tablespoon Worcestershire sauce
1 tablespoon sherry
1/8 teaspoon cayenne pepper
dill pickle (optional)
4—5 slices hot buttered toast

1. Heat the butter in a sauté pan, add onion and green pepper, and sauté for 3 minutes.

2. Add clams, cheese, tomato purée, Worcestershire sauce, sherry and cayenne pepper, and cook for a few minutes until the cheese has melted, stirring all the time.

3. Put a thin slice of dill pickle on each slice of toast and serve the clam mixture on top.

Chicken à la King

Cooked chicken, mushrooms and green pepper heated in a creamy sauce. Serve in pastry shells or on toast or toasted muffins (Serves 5—6)

4 tablespoons butter
2 tablespoons finely chopped onion
1 cup sliced mushrooms
1/2 cup diced green pepper
4 tablespoons flour
2 cups chicken stock
3 cups diced cooked chicken
2 pimentos, drained and cut into
    thin strips
3 tablespoons dry sherry

1. Heat the butter in a skillet, add the onion, mushrooms and green pepper, and cook for 5 minutes.

2. Stir in the flour, mix well with the vegetables, then gradually add chicken stock and stir until boiling. Add seasoning and stir over low heat for 5 minutes.

3. Add chicken, pimentos and sherry and heat through.

English Monkey

(Serves 4)

1 cup milk
1 cup breadcrumbs
1 cup grated Cheddar or American
  cheese
1/2 teaspoon salt
1/4 teaspoon paprika pepper
1/8 teaspoon dry mustard
1 teaspoon Worcestershire sauce
1 egg
4 slices hot buttered toast

1. Put the milk, breadcrumbs and cheese into the top of a double boiler. Stir over hot water until the cheese has melted.

2. Add seasoning, Worcestershire sauce and beaten egg. Cook for 1 minute, stirring all the time, then pour over the toast.

Ham and Pineapple Toast

(Serves 4)

1.1/2 cups ground, cooked ham
1 teaspoon prepared mustard
1/8 teaspoon cayenne pepper
1—2 tablespoons mayonnaise (see p. 24)
4 slices canned pineapple
4 slices hot, lightly buttered toast or
  hamburger rolls

Pre-heat oven to 400°F

1. Season the ham with mustard and pepper and add just enough mayonnaise to bind.

2. Arrange slices of pineapple in an ovenproof pan, pile the ham mixture in a mound on top and heat through in a moderately hot oven for about 5—7 minutes.

3. Serve on lightly buttered hot toast or on halves of toasted hamburger rolls.

QUICK PIES

Squash and Cheese Pie

A supply of baked pie shells in the deep freeze often solves the problem of a snack meal. The filling for this pie consists of squash covered with a fluffy cheese sauce, garnished with slices of tomato and bacon rolls (Serves 4)

3 cups cooked, drained squash
1—8 inch baked pie shell
nutmeg
1 cup cream sauce
1 cup grated cheese
1 egg
2 tomatoes, peeled and sliced
bacon rolls

Pre-heat oven to 400°F Mark 6

1. Cut the well drained squash into cubes and arrange in the pastry shell. Sprinkle with salt, pepper and nutmeg.

2. Make the sauce, add most of the cheese, egg yolk and fold in the stiffly beaten egg white. Pour sauce over the squash.

3. Arrange slices of tomato around the edge and sprinkle the remaining cheese in the middle.

4. Bake for about 15 minutes in a moderately hot oven.

5. Garnish with broiled bacon rolls.

Egg and Shrimp Pie

Slices of egg arranged in a pie shell and covered with a creamy shrimp sauce (Serves 4)

6 eggs
1—8 inch baked pie shell
1 tablespoon butter
1 teaspoon prepared mustard
1.1/2 cups fresh or 1 package frozen
**   shrimps**
1/2 cup cream sauce
1 tablespoon chopped parsley
2 tablespoons grated cheese

Pre-heat broiler

1. Boil the eggs for 7 minutes, then shell and slice carefully. Arrange the slices in the pie shell and sprinkle with a little salt and pepper.

2. Heat the butter in a small pan, add mustard and shrimps and sauté for a few minutes. Stir in the cream sauce and parsley. Check the seasoning and pour the sauce over the eggs.

3. Sprinkle with cheese and brown under a hot broiler.

Sweetcorn and Cheese Pie

1 cup cottage cheese
1/2 cup grated Parmesan cheese
1 can (12 oz) corn
1/4 teaspoon paprika
1 canned pimento, chopped
1 cup cooked peas
1 eight-inch baked pie shell
2 tomatoes, peeled and sliced

Pre-heat oven to 375°F

(Serves 4—5)

1. Combine cottage cheese, Parmesan and drained corn. Season with salt, pepper and paprika and add pimento and peas. If the mixture is a little stiff, add some of the liquor drained from the corn.

2. Pour into the pie shell and arrange slices of tomato around the edge.

3. Bake for about 15 minutes in a moderate oven.

Kidney and Mushroom Saute

A delicious mixture of kidneys, mushrooms and celery in red wine which takes about 10—15 minutes to cook. For a supper snack serve with a green salad or in a border of cooked rice if you need something a little more substantial (Serves 4)

4 tablespoons butter
2 tablespoons finely chopped shallots
1 cup finely chopped celery
4 small veal kidneys, skinned and cored
1 cup sliced mushrooms
2 tablespoons finely chopped parsley
1/2 cup dry red wine
1/4 teaspoon dry mustard
1 cup canned beef gravy

1. Heat the butter in a skillet and sauté the shallots and celery until the shallots begin to soften.

2. Add kidneys, cut into small pieces, and cook quickly until browned-—about 5 minutes.

3. Add mushrooms, parsley, the wine mixed with the mustard, seasoning and gravy. Bring to the boil and cook gently for 3—4 minutes.

Glazed Mushrooms and Ham

Mushrooms, glazed in butter and sugar and served with ham (Serves 4)

1/4 cup butter
1/3 cup brown sugar
1 teaspoon flour
4 cups thickly sliced mushrooms
1/4 teaspoon grated nutmeg
1/4 teaspoon ground mace
4—6 slices cooked ham
3 tablespoons sherry

1. Melt the butter in a pan, add sugar and flour mixed together, and stir over low heat until the sugar has melted.

2. Add mushrooms, nutmeg and mace. Cover and cook very slowly for 5 minutes.

3. Uncover, arrange the ham over the mushrooms and increase the heat just long enough for the ham to heat through.

4. Add the sherry and turn upside down on to a hot serving dish.

Mexican Dip

A favorite with the young—cold, cooked frankfurters heated in a tangy tomato dip to make a hot snack (Serves 4)

3 tablespoons ground or very finely
   chopped onion
3 tablespoons white wine vinegar
1/2 cup tomato ketchup
1 teaspoon Worcestershire sauce
juice of 1/2 lemon
1/2 teaspoon paprika pepper
black pepper, salt, sugar
frankfurters

1. Put onion and vinegar into a pan, and simmer for 5 minutes.

2. Add tomato ketchup, Worcestershire sauce and lemon juice. Simmer for a few minutes longer, then add paprika, pepper, salt and sugar to taste.

3. Cut some frankfurters into 2—3 pieces and heat in the dip.

4. Serve with crusty French bread.

Kidneys in Sherry Sauce

Lamb kidneys sautéed in butter and cooked in stock with sherry. Serve with toast, salad or, for a more substantial snack, on buttered rice (Serves 4)

8 lamb kidneys
1/4 cup butter
1 medium sized onion, peeled and
   finely chopped
2 tablespoons flour
1 chicken bouillon cube dissolved in
   1 cup hot water
freshly ground black pepper
2—3 tablespoons dry sherry
chopped parsley
buttered rice, see below

BUTTERED RICE
1 cup long-grained rice
2 cups water
1 teaspoon salt
1 tablespoon butter

1. Skin and remove the core from the kidneys and cut in halves.

2. Heat half the butter in a small skillet, add the kidney and sauté for 2—3 minutes, then remove from the pan.

3. Add the remaining butter to the pan, add the onion and cook until soft and lightly browned.

4. Replace the kidneys, sprinkle with the flour and blend it carefully with the fat. Stir in the hot stock and continue stirring until boiling. Simmer for 5 minutes. Add salt and pepper to taste and the sherry.

5. Serve sprinkled with parsley.

BUTTERED RICE

1. Butter a pan with a tightly fitting lid and put in the rice, water and salt. Bring to a boil, stir once, put on the lid and simmer over a low heat for 12—15 minutes. Do not stir or remove the lid at this stage.

2. When all the liquid has been absorbed, remove from heat and leave for a few minutes, then add the butter and toss with a fork.

Cheese Crisp

(Serves 4)

6 Graham crackers
2 oz potato chips
6 tablespoons butter
1/2 cup cooked rice
1 cup cream cheese
2 tablespoons chopped gherkins
4 tablespoons mayonnaise (see p. 24)
seasoning
a few thin slices cucumber
paprika

1. Put the crackers and potato chips between greaseproof paper and crush with a rolling pin. Add the melted butter, mix well and press into an 8 inch pie plate. Set aside to chill.

2. Mix the rice, cream cheese and gherkins, add mayonnaise and season to taste.

3. Fill the pie dish. Then garnish with twists of cucumber and sprinkle with paprika.

Note
For variety, try flaked cooked fish instead of cheese.

Sausage and Apple Snack

Apple rings arranged on sausage meat patties and garnished with bacon rolls (Serves 6)

1 lb sausage meat
2 tablespoons chopped parsley
1/2 teaspoon curry powder
1/2 teaspoon mixed herbs
2 tablespoons flour
butter
2 dessert apples
6 thin slices bacon
a few sprigs of parsley
toast

1. Combine sausage meat, parsley, curry powder herbs and seasoning, and shape into 6 patties.

2. Coat lightly with flour and fry in butter for about 5 minutes on each side. Remove from the pan and keep hot.

3. Core but do not peel the apples, cut each into three slices and fry for about 2 minutes on each side.

4. Roll up the bacon, put on to a skewer and fry or broil.

5. Put the sausage patties on a serving dish with an apple ring on top. Arrange the bacon rolls in the center and garnish with parsley. Serve with hot toast.

Salmon and Cheese Rolls

(Serves 4)

1 small can salmon
1 package frozen peas
1 small can evaporated milk
lemon juice
4 hamburger rolls
butter
4 slices American or processed cheese

1. Drain and flake the fish. Add peas and evaporated milk and season with salt, pepper and lemon juice. Stir over low heat until the mixture is smooth and creamy.

2. Split the rolls, spread with butter and put a slice of cheese on one half of each bap.

3. Pile some of the hot fish mixture on top and cover with the other half of the roll. Serve at once.

Bacon Crust Pie

BACON CRUST
1 lb cooked lean ham, finely chopped
    or ground
1 small can tomato purée
1/2 cup breadcrumbs
1 small onion, peeled and chopped
2 tablespoons chopped green pepper

FILLING
1 cup rice, cooked
1 small can tomato purée
1.1/2 cups grated cheese

Pre-heat oven to 375°F
Pre-heat broiler

An unusual bacon crust filled with a mixture of rice and cheese (Serves 4)

1. Mix all the ingredients for the crust, knead well and press into an 8-9 inch pie plate. Flute the edges with the fingers.

2. Combine the rice and tomato purée, and add seasoning to taste. Add most of the grated cheese, and spoon into the bacon shell.

3. Cover with greased paper, and bake for 15 minutes.

4. Remove the paper, sprinkle the remaining cheese on top and brown lightly under a hot broiler.

Cheese Pasties

PASTA PASTRY
2 cups flour
1/2 teaspoon salt
1/4 cup butter or margarine
lukewarm water to mix

FILLING
1/4 cup butter or margarine
1.1/2 cups grated cheese
1 egg

Pasta pastry, cut into rounds, filled with cheese and fried in deep fat (Serves 4)

1. To make pastry, sift the flour and salt, rub in the butter and add enough water to make a soft but not sticky dough. Knead into a ball, cover and leave for about 1 hour.

2. To make the filling, beat the butter until soft. Then beat in most of the cheese, beaten egg and seasoning.

3. Roll out the dough very thinly, cut into rounds with a serrated cutter, about 2.1/2 inches in diameter.

4. Put a little of the cheese mixture on each round of dough, damp the edge and fold over, pressing the edges well together.

5. Fry in deep fat until well browned. Drain and serve sprinkled with the remaining cheese.

Cheese and Bacon Supper Pie

2 tablespoons butter
1 small onion, peeled and chopped
4 slices bacon, diced
2 cups cottage cheese
2 eggs
1 teaspoon mustard
1 baked 8-inch pie shell
chopped parsley
1 tomato

Pre-heat oven to 375°F Mark 5

A baked pie shell makes this a quick snack. It has a filling of cottage cheese flavored with bacon (Serves 4)

1. Heat the butter and sauté the onion until just soft. Add bacon and fry until crisp.

2. Sieve the cheese. Add the beaten eggs, bacon, onion and mustard. Season carefully with a little salt and pepper, and mix well.

3. Turn into the pie shell and bake for about 20 minutes or until the filling is firm and golden brown.

4. Sprinkle with parsley, and garnish with wedges of tomato.

Frankfurter Hash

Frankfurters and hard-boiled eggs heated in mushroom soup. Cooked meat, poultry or hamburgers could be served in the same way (Serves 4)

1 can (about 10 oz) cream of
    mushroom soup
2—3 tablespoons light cream
1.1/2 cups cubed frankfurters
2 hard-boiled eggs, chopped
a pinch of basil or thyme
1 teaspoon chopped parsley

1. Put the mushroom soup into a pan over low heat and add all the other ingredients.

2. Stir until the mixture is hot, then serve on hot toast or corn bread.

Potato Burgers

Hamburgers sandwiched between fried potato cakes (Serves 4)

1 lb cooked mashed potato (2.1/4
    cups)
1 teaspoon chopped chives
black pepper, nutmeg
butter for frying
1 cup ground raw beef
1/2 small onion, peeled and finely
    chopped
1 teaspoon prepared horseradish
egg to bind

1. Combine the potato and chives, with salt, pepper and a pinch of nutmeg. Roll out on a floured surface about 1/4 inch thick and cut into 2.1/2—3 inch rounds. Fry in hot butter until brown on both sides. Remove from pan and keep hot.

2. Combine the beef, onion and horseradish, season and add enough egg to bind. Form into flat rounds the same size as the potato cakes. Fry until cooked and brown on both sides—aboout 5—7 minutes.

3. Sandwich a hamburger between two potato cakes and serve at once.

Ham and Potato Cakes

Slices of ham and cheese served on potato cakes (Serves 4)

1 lb cooked mashed potato
2 tablespoons butter
milk
4 slices ham
4 slices Gruyère or processed cheese
chopped parsley

Pre-heat oven to 400°F

1. Season the potatoes well with salt and pepper. Add 1 tablespoon butter and a little milk if required. Shape into four flat cakes. Put on to a greased baking pan, dot with the remaining butter and brown in oven.

2. Top with a slice of ham and cheese, and return to the oven until the cheese begins to melt.

3. Sprinkle with parsley before serving.